Everyday Knowledge

JAMES CUMMINS

DOS MADRES

2025

DOS MADRES PRESS INC.

P.O. Box 294, Loveland, Ohio 45140
www.dosmadres.com   editor@dosmadres.com

Dos Madres is dedicated to the belief that the small press is essential to the vitality of contemporary literature as a carrier of the new voice, as well as the older, sometimes forgotten voices of the past. And in an ever more virtual world, to the creation of fine books pleasing to the eye and hand.

Dos Madres is named in honor of Vera Murphy and Libbie Hughes, the "Dos Madres" whose contributions have made this press possible.

Dos Madres Press, Inc. is an Ohio Not For Profit Corporation and a 501 (c) (3) qualified public charity. Contributions are tax deductible.

Executive Editor: Robert J. Murphy

Illustration & Book Design: Elizabeth H. Murphy
www.illusionstudios.net

Typeset in Adobe Garamond Pro & American Typewriter
ISBN 978-1-962847-21-6
Library of Congress Control Number: 2025931771

for Maureen

Table of Contents

I

II

III

IV

Everyday Knowledge

I

*"Life at my age is not easy,
but spring is beautiful and so is love."*

—Freud, letter to Hilda Doolittle

Song for K.

I daydream about us in a French movie, maybe *Claire's Knee*.
You have a place on Lake Geneva, and I come to visit you
from my place farther up the lake. I have a small boat—
an unprepossessing, non-Homeric boat—
and we drink white wine in the garden at a white table,
while talking leisurely about life, love, sex, more sex.
Somebody's niece tumbles by with her boyfriend,
a rowdy footballer who stands for youth and untamed passion.
She's experimenting with American hair styles;
you tell her how to say "ponytail" in French.
I smile benignly, pour another glass of white wine.
After they leave, you imply I wanted to touch her breasts.
I don't deny this. It's France, after all. You smile.
We continue to talk languorously about life, love, sex.
The maid brings us a light lunch; we are surrounded by flowers.
Then we either go to bed, or I return to my little boat.
The French are pretty casual about sex, but I'm not French,
so I climb into my boat as you say, 'Tomorrow?'
and I say 'Of course' and wave good-bye.
It's a daydream, and I'm really sitting on my porch,
drinking lemonade and thinking about cutting the grass.
But I close my eyes for a moment—and there you are again,
waving, as I come to visit you in my boat.

Dancer and Dance

When he was young, he thought his narcissism
was anguish; but it was just narcissism.
Everyone's in some kind of anguish or other—
or do the Protestants merely suffer?
Protestants buy things; it helps the pain.
Catholics buy things, too, but it doesn't help—

Protestants don't get how things "accrue."
They gain their purchase on the earth
by purchasing it. No vestments, incense,
mumbling over wafers, in the economical church—
no folderol, no magic tricks, no ghosts.
And certainly no "Stations of the Cross,"

reminding you every Sunday of anguish
you couldn't conceive of. Not to mention
the shit you had to go through to be a saint—
a woman carrying her eyeballs on a plate?
Most of all, that body on the cross,
writhing in agony if you looked more closely.

Back then, when they crucified you,
they drove the nails into your wrists & ankles—
otherwise, your flesh ripped away
& the heap of you ended up on the ground.
They wanted you to die, but in agony,
on rough wood, not on a breast of dirt.

Of course, if they wanted you to die faster,
they broke your legs at the knee—that way,
you'd be lucky if you lasted half an hour.
But suffering is different from anguish—
anyone familiar with both knows that.
Suffering touches the body, but anguish

torches the soul. When they crucified Peter,
they turned the old man upside-down.
They said they wanted him to reconsider;
but really, they just wanted to kill somebody
that morning. A bright cheerful morning,
the pictures say, if you didn't mind seeing

a gray-haired man, somebody's dad or grandpa,
getting nailed upside-down to some wood.
I suppose, at the end, the old fisherman
got what he desired. You could even say
he saw it coming, spreading his arms out wide,
knowing he was the one that got away.

Teaching Film Noir

"*Existentialism,*" I tell my film noir class the first day,
"is a good starter philosophy, like a small house you buy
when you first get married. Maybe you have a child
there, even as you dream of moving to a bigger house
in a better neighborhood—but all the while you take
responsibility for your actions in an absurd universe."
Then I mention a jumble of things about 1945, and the French.

A critic taught me all I knew about the movies
before I let the movies themselves begin to teach me.
I remember one passage, about *Rebel Without a Cause,*
where he describes the teenagers walking into a planetarium,
then lying back in their seats as they stare at the universe—
passively accepting, as a given, that the heavens wheel by
without relation to one another, and we drift alone
in the cosmic sea of ourselves. I begin my lecture:
"In a post-Nietzschean world the ego is a succession
of identities, of masks, as it were"—then watch
as post-Nietzschean anxiety squeezes essence
from existence in stoic, Bible Belt style.

I'm from the Midwest; I know my audience.
You have to drop terms like "mask" and "Nietzsche,"
establish your campus street-cred as you lure them
into a sketchy neighborhood of ideas, to mug them
with the notion they're maybe not the identities
they assumed earlier that morning at McDonald's.
Of course, "God" eventually staggers into the picture.
Many of them, in fact, are hoping God will actually walk in

and gently remonstrate with me, while two buffed angels
in white T-shirts labeled "Security" lift me and carry me off,
wildly gesticulating, like a distraught Cary Grant.
A girl is wearing a James Dean sweatshirt, but she looks
as confused as the others. A thought occurs to me:
I should wear an eyepatch like Nicholas Ray.

I met Nick Ray, the director of *Rebel*, in Berkeley
once, at a conference for Hollywood *auteurs*.
Ray was an old pirate: black eye patch, creative fire
whistling around us like a sword. He had no use for poets,
or to be honest, teachers; but he looked me in the eye
as he shook my hand, and I looked him in the eye, too,
the good one, and saw he was mad as a hatter,
therefore trustworthy. I'm older than Ray was then.
I don't feel older, but then I don't smoke.
It's amazing to me we can even see the '50s now
through the dome of their cigarette smoke.
I'd say lung cancer won't get me, as it got Ray,
but that might tempt the gods, my whimsical gods,
who remonstrate with me morning and evening.
The succession of identities (*"masks, as it were"*)
I put on daily myself, is a long lifeline of mirrors,
which alone accounts for much of my students' *dread*.
(Eventually they will come to love the word "dread.")

I'm not unlike that hoary ploy of dominoes,
an intricate design taking up the floor of a high school gym
that television crews come out to film for a feature
to fill some time on the local news. With great fanfare
the first block goes down—the camera darts and scans,
ooo-ing and *aah*-ing along, presenting to viewers

of the *Six O'Clock News*, most of them parents,
this neighborly example of the butterfly effect—
which finally reveals the date and time of a local church's
annual spaghetti dinner for the poor.

We watch the movies together in class. I tell them
The Maltese Falcon is a filmed play, but they *want* to talk
about betrayal, *hubris*. I mention that Glenn Ford's wife
in *The Big Heat* is Marlon Brando's big sister, Jocelyn.
They ask, "Who's Marlon Brando?" (I tell them that was
just an aside, but they're welcome to "Google" him.)
They're astonished at Mike Hammer's bare-knuckle sadism
in *Kiss Me Deadly,* or the torture scene in *The Big Combo,*
these children who've seen 10,000 murders already;
and they're actually shocked at what Joseph H. Lewis
said Mr. Brown was doing, as he knelt behind Jean Wallace—
forget about Cornel Wilde, her "real life" husband, screaming.

I've alienated my film noir students with *alienation*,
except for one boy who wants to talk philosophy,
so we get coffee and I see he's not all that interested
in grades, but is more like me when I was his age:
a head bouncing wildly in the first thunderstorms
of thought. "It's like—it's like—*King Lear!*"
he keeps saying; and I refrain from pointing out
that everything is like *King Lear.*

Nicholas Ray attended the University of Wisconsin
as Raymond Nicholas Kienzle, never imagining then
that he would divorce Gloria Grahame in 1952
after surprising her in bed with his 13-year-old son, Tony.
(Gloria and Tony married as soon as they could;

Tony always said Gloria was "the love of his life.")
Thornton Wilder and Frank Lloyd Wright
were the gods gaffing Ray's thunderstorms of thought.
Do fathers teach us how to *work* while we live
inside our mothers for nine months? How to get *out?*
My students glow with the rudest of health.
Not liking something is sufficient thinking for them—
they don't feel the need to conceive of what they're not.
The *Is*-ness of the Midwest stems from planting,
the cycle of the seasons still a yearly becoming,
demanding responsibilities, not choices.
But now the young man, in his eager turbulence,
becomes the way the others tune me in: he lets himself
be laughed at, while the others learn from this.

One morning I put on a black leather eye patch,
look for a rubber sword in the attic. I strut and rave
before them, wanting to curse, call them names—
but the Dean, you know. So speak code instead:
"Our demons aren't our demons anymore—
they've been bought off! *They've been bought off!*"
A few are amused; a few uncomfortable; a few alarmed.
A girl in the front row writes the word *"absurd"*
in a notebook spangled with glitter and glued-on jewels.
I begin to worry I've walked the plank, but then
some of them laugh out loud, then a few more
begin to chant, then a few more join in,
as if they're prepping for the final:
"You're not what you believe, but what you do!"

Why Midwestern Kids Stand Up

1

I saw Ted Williams play several times
in Cleveland's Municipal Stadium when I was eight;
the game I best remember, a first-inning single
went through Ted's legs for an error.
The boos & catcalls began; Ted was humiliated.
I was reading everything I could handle then,
mispronouncing words like "*char*-acter" and "*i*-doit"
but soldiering on, trying to connect the words
with the things I saw around me every day.
I had a revelation now: I understood the description
of a neck turning "brick red"—Ted's neck
turned brick red as he pounded his glove in frustration.

We sat in the second row of the left-field bleachers.
I was directly on the foul line when Jimmy Piersall
led off the next inning with a home run.
He hit a line drive I watched from home plate
that never wavered on or off the foul line
until it reached our seats. My father stood up,
prepared to catch it, and I stood up with him.
I was eight. I stood up because my father stood up.
My father played baseball in the Navy;
he won a roller-skating trophy in Oakland, California,
before being deployed on the *USS Intrepid.*
He was a medic who reached up into the stump
of a man's leg blown off in a *kamikaze* attack,
to clamp the artery and save the man's life.

I didn't really understand these things yet;
I just knew he wasn't afraid of a line drive,
so I wasn't either. I waited for the ball to arrive,
thrilled at the possibility of proving myself;
I'm sure my father waited to protect me.

The ball was caught cleanly by the man sitting
in the first-row seat in front of me—deftly,
gracefully. I was disappointed but impressed.
I looked around the stadium: all the men (the crowd
was mostly men) were wearing white shirts—
short-sleeved white shirts because it was summer.
I had the feeling that all the men worked in offices,
or sold food products to groceries as my father did;
I had the feeling any one of them would stand up
to catch a line drive or probe a blown-off stump.

2

Years later I'm walking up a flight of steps to a bar.
With me are my best friend, David, his friend, Alison,
from Indiana, where I'd lived five years growing up,
and David's friend from childhood, Allan, also from Brooklyn.
Suddenly someone bumped me—I thought mistakenly—
so I apologized because I'm from the Midwest.
But then he bumped me again, almost causing me to fall,
then came at me swinging roundhouse punches like—
pardon me for saying this—a girl. Easy enough
to step inside and grab him by the throat, which I did,
then bang his head against a gate until he dropped
his hands. He said, "This is strange behavior for you."
I thought the guy was crazy, and said so, then let go,

continued to the bar. We thought the spectacle was over;
the four of us found a table, got menus, ordered drinks.

Then suddenly the guy appears again, begins to whine
and stomp his feet, threatening me. My Brooklyn friends
just as suddenly disappear, to find "a bouncer."
(It's an upscale bar for law students; there was no "bouncer.")
But who protects me? Alison stands up, threatens
to kick his balls up through his shoulder blades;
around us three or four young men push out their chairs.

The Life Alongside This Life

The answer to every riddle lies inside our bodies:
life, the continuation of life …
I wake at three a.m. with the guilt of it,
the guilt of life. I haven't asked my body the question.

Exactly my age, but a month—and you lie
in a different city, asking yourself over and over,
Why? The question for all of us is *When?*
but instead we ask our bodies *Why?*

because we're afraid, and afraid to be afraid.
Why? keeps a part of us in the equation, in the action,
a part of what we are, in the face of the howling
that we call "the wind" to frame it.

Like the door to a cabin in winter in a play:
the characters take turns opening the door—
to get firewood, to check on the animals,
whatever of myriad reasons they can invent,

some Necessity they're obliged to bow to—
just to check it out, the howling, their bodies strong,
no matter their fear—to check it out, endure it,
then to stomp their way back into the warmth.

Stranger on the Shore

after John Koethe's "The Divinity Within"

The "divinity within" is the result of a chemical process
that often engenders "the peace that passeth understanding";
and is sometimes mistaken as a "theophany" or visitation
by whatever god turns you on by battering your heart.
It's not. Or rather, it is, but first you'd have to redefine
the word "god." "He" is not gender-specific, and certainly
not capitalized & he doesn't reside "up there" somewhere.
"God" is merely a projection of our best & worst designs.
I see now this is going to involve a discussion of "metaphor,"
but that's okay because, when you get down to it, everything
resembles everything else that isn't you, by not resembling
anything else, except mysteriously. I know it's complicated.
"God" is just a metaphor for the divinity within—the catch is,
we've hung on to the wrong divinity like a dog with a rag.

You've got to let the rag go. Let the dog run, be a dog!
In fact, the ones who don't understand "the divinity within"
are the ones who think a thing is different from another thing,
and believe the final form of each "thing" is the acquisition of it.
I don't want to get into "the Mysteries" here, and all that—
though googling "Eleusinian" & pondering the result for a while
wouldn't be a terrible waste of time—or just "Dionysus," maybe—
and Emerson, of course, had the whole thing down pat—
the point is, "God" was a projection of our concept of power,
which for various economic reasons that benefitted many,
& a few psychological ones that were, to say the least, a mixed bag,
we ensconced him "up there" to minimize any divine meddling
in our daily business, except when we needed some help.

Good people saw him as good; bad people saw him as their parents.
Sadly, bad parenting has held its sway over the course of time;
economic odds favor it. Really, the story of Western Civilization
is lousy parenting. But hopefully, someone's working on that.

If we can't reduce "the divinity within" to mere chemical process—
though "mere" is a loaded term here—we can study descriptions
of the feeling that floods us with connectedness and tolerance.
D. T. Suzuki said *satori* was doing all the usual daily tasks, just
one inch off the ground; Buddha pictured a flowering in the brain.
Only the monotheisms think a god outside the body possesses you:
a sort of mystical homoeroticism, resulting in hatred of women
and a bonding with like-minded souls who're also afraid of them.
Maybe "hatred" is too strong: "misunderstandings abounding"—
how's that? Unfortunately, misunderstandings on the part
of muscular 190-pound gym machine lunatics wearing wifebeaters,
who mistake divinity as the expression of their physical narcissism,
can wreak havoc on 120-pound bodies, no matter how fit or alluring.

Ann Landers said whatever turns you on—drugs, Jesus, love—
is okay as long as you bring it back home to the wife. Wifebeaters,
listen up! I prefer what a poet said: *"What makes a life divine isn't
its perfection or its power, but its estrangement from the world
and the reflection of itself in all it sees."* Metaphor translates us
into the world, and the world into us, then leaves us high
and dry on a rock, pondering our estrangement in peace.
We are the "godlike" expressions of the world, not the reverse;
we've always held the world in a confused embrace. Or it has us.
Think of Acker Bilk strolling a lonely beach at sunset, blowing
his solitary clarinet until the walls come down, but quietly.

No Virgil

You say you know I 'hate' men because
'somewhere deep down' I hate myself—
first-year psych. First world, too.
I'm working on this, but it'll take
more than one lifetime to figure out:
I'm going to have to come back
two or three times as a cockroach.
Which isn't so bad—cockroaches
are the great survivors, after all—
but hey, you're still a cockroach.

I've found through personal experience
you can't heal the sick or the wounded.
I realize this wouldn't condemn me
to three tours in *Cockroachistan* but I
didn't bring my whole arsenal to the fight:
I replaced Love with Care. I was a liar.

Men like me who are liars should meet
Dante and his friend in a bar where lights
bounce off red plastic like the fires of Hell.
So why don't you kill yourself, you ask.
A good question but a bit naive, I could say.
There are extenuating circumstances,
not least that those you care about either
wouldn't understand or need the money.

My dad lived in a kind of hell of silence.
When I was eight I was so full of thoughts.
We'd go for walks in the clear ice-cold
Cleveland nights, and he wouldn't say a word.
I would whistle, sharply, perfectly, I thought,
to show him how good a whistler I was.
Not a word. Never a word. I finally got that

he had a lot on his mind, too: husband, son,
father, middle-class wage earner with never
enough wages. A white collar was important
to my mother's family, and I guess to him, too.
He even converted, for show, to Catholicism;
I remember him kneeling in humiliation.

He knelt one other time, in a tent, in mud,
in a driving rainstorm in Newark, Ohio,
as he and I buried his father. I wanted to
embrace him then—want to embrace him now—
but it's not possible. I didn't bury him but
fed him to the flames of a crematorium,
with no Dante to interpret his silence,
and no Virgil to guide him on his way.

II

*"Far from marveling at the object,
objective thought must treat it ironically."*

—Gaston Bachelard

On The Road Ode

In the Ocala Holiday Inn
the hips and thighs thumping
the 'free Continental breakfast bar'
are even yet the humanity
the poet spoke of so movingly,
though the total poundage itself
stays much movement at all;
and mouths spit bits of food,
demanding seconds, with coffee.
A woman in a cashmere coat
sips fresh-squeezed orange juice
from a clear plastic cup
as she imagines these beasts
scooping water from a hole;
a man who's sure God loves him
makes a secret sign over his tray.
Behind a Lazy Susan rack
of local real-estate pamphlets,
a mother in a Dallas Cowboys jersey
speaks to her daughter calmly
as she spreads cream cheese
on their microwaved bagels;
and an Appalachian man—
smoker, long hair short at his ears—
gazes shyly at a wife made weary
by all his good times. Their
burr-headed son, ten, chews
his cereal with a thoughtful look.

An American Folly

In 1906, Mary Astor Paul
was seventeen and Philadelphia's own.
The Gilded Age had lost a little gilt—
and *cotillion* some magic it once held—
but seventeen-year-old Mary had a plan.
So many young beauties had paved the way
for coming out among the privileged few,
hawking their *derrieres*, their ankles, breasts,
beneath the richest linens, Chinese silks,
and provenance-murky diamonds and pearls.
Somewhere along the way we've lost Beauty—
so Mary thought—and thought to win it back.
Somehow we've lost the virginal, the Pure.
What kind of signal could she send to them,
to make her coming out become unique?

One afternoon as Mary pondered this,
she watched two robins sharing a birdbath.
She felt the laziness of early spring,
relaxing in the back garden with tea.
Someone had left a box of digging tools
near the glass-topped stand holding her cup;
and on its flap a yellow butterfly,
orange and blue marks on its trembling wings,
shook like a tiny violet in a breeze.
Its delicate beauty—its nearness, too—
she didn't know what to admire more:
its color or tenacity. The breeze
was slight but fluttered the small wings; and yet
the little being clung; it stared at her.
The penny dropped and Mary raced inside.

One thing about the rich, they have a lot
of books. They have to—it's all part of it:
books bespeak a different kind of wealth.
Mary pulled down a book on butterflies,
then another, and another, then two more.
She jumped from book to book the way a girl
might jump from stone to stone across a stream.
When Mary left the room, her plan in place
(she left the butler to re-shelve the books),
she set to work to realize her vision:
ten thousand butterflies cascading down—
extravagant colors and wings like breath—
delighting Philadelphia's Elect.
Only seventeen, yet she got it done—
drew up the plan and servants did the rest.

The proverbs that we live by tell our tales.
'The best laid plans of mice and men" is one;
"The devil's in the details" is another;
but that day was the site for devilish glee.
The cords that held the bugs were strung indoors—
some say the too-high nets reached too-hot lights,
and others that the room itself lacked air—
but when the nets opened, the bugs were dead.
They twisted down like helicopter seeds,
sticking onto hair, *decolletage,* pomade,
clogging plates of beef, bread, custards, tea—
Brazilian butterflies in thousands fell
like dead manna into silver tureens
and gleaming platters holding veal and fish—
half-in, half-out of glasses of champagne.

Some people with phobias vomited;
some passed out under bowls of soup that tipped.
Some held lace handkerchiefs against their lips,
and murmured grim apologies, then ran,
their boots and slippers crunching husks of bugs,
sometimes slipping on wings or insect grit.
Mary surveyed this tragic battleground
like a general who's all too well aware
of who's at fault. Maybe she remembered—
how could she not?—this absurd debacle
all her life; and then again, maybe not.
Almost four decades later Mary Paul
ran a French Resistance cell in Paris,
a brave woman who knew a lot about
how human vanity leads to mass death.

Between the Lines

after *A Moveable Feast*

We only have Papa's account of this,
that Scott Fitzgerald asked him to weigh in
with 'absolute honesty' on the question
that filled Fitzgerald's heart with fear and dread:
was he big enough? Was he man enough
to please a woman? "Zelda?" his friend asked.
Scott nodded, surprised. "Yes, Zelda. Who else?"

It's clear Hemingway wants to reassure
his buddy with a comforting response,
so he fumes at women. "They're all alike.
They only want to crush a man—it's true!
Crazy Zelda's just trying to kill you."
Scott looks up from his cherry tart:
"You don't know anything about Zelda!"
Hemingway backs off that one like hot
potato soup dropped in his lap by one
of old Michaud's careless waiters.
He lifts a spoon to his own cherry tart;
outside he hears the racket of a car.

"Have you tried a pillow?" he asks quietly.
"You've got to get some purchase on that slope.
A pillow can facilitate your mount."
Scott stares at his wine glass. "I never know
whether I'm in or not," he says.
"When I ask, she gets disgusted. Cries."

At this Ernie almost upsets his wine.
He can't abide a woman's tears—he can't!
They've tried their tricks on him and found
he's what a man should be: a stone.
They've tried the "too small" line before;
and sure, he'd spent some sleepless nights
reviewing his performance in the sack—
but if a woman can't be satisfied,
he wasn't going to take that on himself!

"What if she's right? What if I'm just too small?"
Scott's question broke through his friend's reverie—
who slammed his hand down on the table top.
"Let's check it out! Let's go to *le water.*"
Scott suddenly looked blank. "Well, I don't know,"
he said. "I mean, they do that in Pigalle—"
"For Christ's sake, Scottie, I don't want your balls!
You asked for my 'absolute honesty.'
Let's get some sort of assessment in hand.
So to speak." Scott sighed, "Yes, so to speak ..."

"Michaud!" Now Hemingway was all business.
"Michaud, come help us out? And bring Pierre."
Scott looked alarmed. "Ernie, old man—old sport—"
But Hemingway brushed all dissent aside.
"Don't 'old sport' me! Save it for your prose.
Come on, we'll have a good old show-and-tell—
you show, the rest of us will tell." But Scott
held firm, and only he and Hemingway
repaired to *le water*, the dank men's room,
where Scott undid his belt and dropped his *trou.*

Now Hemingway's a bit unclear about
what happens next: we're given to believe
he checks Scott out, and then they reappear,
attabler, with their cherry tarts and wine.
But old Michaud fills in the blanks for us.
One of his waiters, Francois, had the runs
that day, and so was seated in a stall
reading *Le Monde* when Scott pulled down his pants.
Francois' account is somewhat vague because
he had to stare through a narrow crack;
but evidently Hemingway squatted,
then got down on all fours so he could find
the 'angle of the dangle' as he called it.
And Francois swears he heard him say,
"Pull it a couple times, see if it moves."
But Francois' English wasn't, say, the King's.

Then they're sitting above their lunch again,
and Ernie is expansive. This might mean
that what Scott showed his friend in *le water*
wouldn't keep his friend awake at night.
"It's not the size that counts; it's the motion—"
the friend was one big friendly smile.
"Let's hit the Louvre and size the statues up.
You'll see—their scale is pretty much the truth."
A frightening image flared in Scottie's mind:
Ernie measuring statues with a tape.
He stammered out, "I really should get back"—
Was Ernie more obsessed with ... *that* ... than he?

"Zelda can't make you any more a man
than some whore you could pick up in Pigalle.
A pal can boost your confidence, that's all."
The Louvre was just a short walk from Michaud's,
but Scott was adamant outside the bar.
They let the tarts settle and had a smoke;
Ernie studied his pal as they stood there.
Was that the problem then? Scott was a poof?
He'd never judge a friend. Then he thought
maybe he'd pushed him too far for one day.
"I guess you're right," he said, "it's getting late.
The Louvre's a project for another day."

Except they did go to the Louvre that day;
and Hemingway explained to Fitzgerald,
"the 'proper measurement of man is man.'"
Scott still had his theories about finance,
how these abstractions can suck out your soul;
and Ernie still thought life a game
between whose lines a man's soul finds its measure.
They stopped at Dingo's on the way back home
to drink *aperitifs* and watch the sun
slip through the pink clouds of a Paris dusk.
Ernie held up his glass to catch the light,
and then intoned, without cracking a smile:
"A *Rosé* is a *Rosé* is a *Rosé*."

The Searchers

John Wayne was a movie icon.
He *was* America: big, tough, white, mean.
Mean in *Red River, Wings of Eagles;*
sweet, young, honorable, in *Stagecoach,*
but still tough. And almost bigger than
the door frame at the end of *The Searchers,*
but not bigger than the sky. He'd learned,
too late, no one's bigger than the sky.

But he never could act, you say, sniffing.
What does acting have to do with an icon?
It's easy to have your mystical visions
in Jersey or Massachusetts: they're small.
But put Whitman and Emerson down
in Montana or Wyoming, see how they do.
It's one thing to stand in Times Square
and wonder about the meaning of life;
it's quite another to realize you're closer
to the Indians you've hunted for years
than you are to the decent Christian folk
celebrating your return to the fold.
Then you step out and look up at the sky:
how can you include so much space
in your heart, let alone in a philosophy?

In 1896, Nicholas Black Elk survived
genocide at Wounded Knee, a slaughter
of old men, women & children—revenge
by white cavalry for the Little Big Horn,

fought two decades earlier and named
'Greasy Grass' by the Oglala Sioux;
there, Nick and his cousin Crazy Horse
wiped out Custer's Seventh Cavalry.

In 1932, after a career as a performer
in Buffalo Bill Cody's Wild West shows,
Nicholas Black Elk, a baptized Christian,
spoke through his son, Ben Black Elk,
to record young Nick's mystical visions
becoming a shaman and a war chief.
In 1956, John Ford gave John Wayne
a film script, a copy of *Black Elk Speaks*,
and the novel by Alan Le May on which
the film was based, saying this was prep:

*It's 1868 and Ethan Edwards will spend
the next five years searching for his niece,
who's probably his daughter, so he can put—
as a kind & gentle Vivien Leigh spells out—
"a bullet in her brain." Everyone involved,
except the niece, agrees this is needed to purify
what's been defiled by a fiendish penetration
of the frontier community's godly whiteness
that the girl never realizes she embodies.*

Nick Black Elk wouldn't speak to whites
for more than fifty years, in movie time.
Decades later, the Irishman Jack Feeney—
aka, Sean Aloysius Ó Fearna, *aka* John Ford,
whose parents emigrated from Galway
and Inis Mor in the Aran Islands—

recorded *his* tale of alienation set in Texas.
The Duke was grateful for indoor plumbing,
while he did his research on white hatred;
but Marion Morrison must have known
something of the power of Nick's visions,
as he studied them in Utah while waiting
for the call to be someone he wasn't.

Pamphlet Included With Gun Purchase

"Guns are just the American response
to the cultural problem of the female ...
A gun in one hand, a half-naked broad in the other—
who cares if they blow you away then,

whoever 'they' are ... Better than worrying
about the mothers, the daughters, the wives—
all the bitches you find at the bottom of a glass ...
Don't hit them, everyone says. Oh hell, hit them.

A woman is a trip-wire, the tantalizing bonus
if you can make it through the field alive;
but the calculator of odds you won't.
A woman watches limbs fly, as a sign.

A woman is the fishing line, not the fish.
You eat the fish, and it gives you pleasure,
but the thrill is in the line wobbling, the bob.
Will she or won't she becomes will you or won't you.

A gun takes care of everything, but be careful
not to fetishize the bullet: you want lots
of bullets, spraying across the room like spunk.
A single bullet is a roulette ball, a chance."

Restraining Order

I think it's the word 'stalker' that gets me.
I'm not stalking anyone, least of all her.
Half the time, I'm not even thinking about her,
until she sees me again, and then it's too late.

I'm not angry about the kids, either. I mean,
I love them and all, but they're so much work;
and frankly, I enjoy the lack of responsibility.
It's like, for once in my life, I have free time.

It's true, I sometimes used the kids to scare her,
to back her off a little, when she got too close.
It's a violent world, I told her, and I meant it,
but I didn't mean I'd contribute to the violence.

She never understood me. She was always too
'hysterical' or whatever they call it nowadays—
jumping to conclusions, never letting me explain.
Can you live with someone who won't let you talk?

She talks the talk now, but I'm walking the walk—
hah! She never got my sense of humor, either.
She always saw something dark in what I said;
dark and nasty, she'd say. But I was only kidding,

most of the time. Unless I was making a point.
I used to just stare at her—so cute back then,
so nervous, inept. Like now, juggling groceries
while she fumbles with her keys at the front door.

Stage Five

It started out as a murder-suicide pact,
but I'm pretty sure I knew all along
I wouldn't be able to pull the trigger again
after I saw her body lying on the floor.
Things seemed different at that moment—
somehow, life itself seemed different.

We still had Stage 4 cancer, or I did;
I still felt sorrow, and loyalty to her;
but suddenly I felt I could do something
with the time I had left—something
important, meaningful, something that
honored that body lying in her blood.

I had no idea what. And I don't say
I was unaware of immediate contingencies—
I had to go on the run, for one thing—
but not until I had cleaned the carpet
with bleach, got a tarp from the garage—
why didn't we do this on the tile floor

of the kitchen, or in the bathroom,
in the tub?—and disposed—it sounds
so cold, so calculating—of the body.
(And sopped up the gallons of blood—
it *seemed* like gallons. And what
does one do with a body, anyway?)

She was so much more than a body,
of course—a vibrant young woman;
a wife, a mother, a career lawyer;
then a middle-aged cancer survivor—
up to a point. But it had come back,
and we'd joked I'd caught it from her.

I stared down at her now—the bullets
had dislodged the 'Locks of Love' wig
she got from Medicare at no charge.
Her still-bald head had a silky shadow—
roots of the ravishing raven tresses
I'd treasured so much in our youth.

Now I pondered those years with pleasure.
We'd made love on the kitchen floor,
in the bathtub, on the sofa, in the car.
Tonight her body looked young again—
unmarred, no blotches or veins—
or perhaps I just couldn't see them.

My pleasure grew, much to my alarm ...
At first I was horrified by my thoughts;
but then—she was my wife, after all—
we'd enjoyed giving each other pleasure.
I knelt and kissed her still-warm buttocks,
gently spread her legs with the gun.

Pentecost

They believe their god rose up from the dead,
exited his Son-of-Man Cave by rolling away a stone,
then floated up into the sky after hanging around
for a few weeks with his squeeze & their *entourage.*

And those followers of his—old biddy gossips!
You could watch the red tongues fluttering
& flapping wildly above their shameless heads!
"Yada, yada," his mother said, shaking hers.

He was a bit of a boor when they got together:
"Stick your hand in my side, go ahead, stick it!
Thumb my holes! Got any dead people I can raise
before my flight?" Guy was a real comedian—

the guy part or the god part, we're not sure—
but the *Good News*-papers smoothed that out.
It would be unseemly to cast him as some sort of
proto-Henny Youngman: "Take my life. Please."

'Heavenly Creatures'

In 1953 New Zealand, two teenage girls, Juliet Hulme, 15, and Pauline Parker, 16, afraid of being separated, murdered Pauline's mother with a brick. After a prison term, Juliet moved to Scotland, changed her name to 'Anne Perry' and became an acclaimed writer of Victorian mysteries. She has sold over 25 million books. In 1994, 'Heavenly Creatures,' Kate Winslet's first film, told the Hulme-Parker story.

Observer: *"When I was young, I saw their pov. Now I feel like the mother."*

Anne Perry: *"It is vital for me to go on exploring moral matters."*

"And I feel like the brick left by the side of the road, alone, picked up by cops & stashed in a box in an evidence room, unused. Never able to forget the feel of flesh and bone as I rose and fell, rose and fell ... I could have been a part of something—a school, a deck! But no, a killer, unable even to say a word in my defense.

A little paint & I could've been
a road, a girl in ruby slippers
could've followed me to safety.
Of course, flying monkeys
would have shit all over us,
but we would have been free!"

Death of an Atheist

All the things that matter must fall away
like clothes before lovemaking
or flesh from the autopsy's scalpel.

Love must fall away; and hate.
Objects must fall away, and memory of objects.
The warmth of hands—all warmth, really,

must fall away, and the fear of cold
must be replaced with a cold welcome.
There is no light, no door; the memory

of light and doors must fall away.
Voices must fall away, even the voices
of loved ones must fall away,

as their faces have already fallen away.
The cries of this world fall away,
and no cries replace them,

no cries of the damned or the grateful;
and the silence that isn't silence falls away.
What remains is a life.

Requiem With Job Jar

after Kim Ki-young's *Hanyo* *["The Housemaid"]*

The day is coming, and no doubt sooner than we think,
when one or the other of us will find the other one dead.
One of us won't much care, but the other one will care a lot.
No abstract preparations for this day will alter the impact;
no plot purchases, insurance policies, display venue costs,
contracted for when the corpse still had a working billfold,
will reassure the finder as they were once meant to do.

And beyond what personal feeling still exists after fifty years,
there will also be the fact that a corpse has suddenly appeared
in the house; and corpses are their own particular thing.
Most people only see a few corpses in their entire lifetime;
and this will probably be the first one they see in their home.
Corpses are by nature disconcerting, but no one is prepared
for the facial expressions left over from life: maybe the eyes
didn't make it all the way closed, or the jaw still tries to speak.
Maybe you have to loosen a hand gripping a blanket.

And the personal narrative that every partner has invented
over the stretch of years can't prepare for this end, either.
It's impossible: maybe you went to bed angry, or oblivious,
but waking up to this already-stiffening bundle of flesh
was the last thing you expected to find in your conjugal bed.
Of course, this assumes you've still been sharing a conjugal bed.
Over the years many things may have driven you to separate rooms:
snoring, mutual disgust, morning breath that begins in the evening,
gas—still, the face of someone you love, or at least once loved,
staring up at you like the head of a dead trout, will move you

to some sort of primitive scream of unthinking horror.
It's probably too much to ask you to gauge your reactions then,
but oddly enough these occasions do have their own protocols.
I bring this up because you'll assess your behavior for weeks.
Did you run? In which direction? If the hallway, was it guilt
that propelled you, because you'd dreamed of this for years?

Guilt is unhealthy; it's normal to imagine a partner's demise.
It's an end-of-life "settling," just like when you both "settled"
to begin with: the person you *wanted* to marry unfortunately
was taken, or otherwise unavailable, and you found you could
learn to enjoy sex with just about anyone; so before *this* ship
sailed, too, you both made practical & reasonable decisions.

But sitting here in the corner with your wrist in your mouth
isn't going to take care of this suddenly-appearing job jar.
You must notify people. *The children!* They'll want to know.
Fortunately, you've outlived most of the relatives on either side.
Do you have to call the coroner's office? Or just dial 911?
An ambulance! Oh shit, *an obituary!* Your wrist falls away
as you stare at the bundle in a new light. *Christ, even in death ...*

Veterans' Day

He sits on the porch getting eaten by mosquitoes,
swatting, waving, musing on Corregidor, Guadalcanal:
hot, humid, dank; smothering blankets of mosquitoes;
and Japanese fanatics waiting and willing to die.
That's worth a tattoo, to catch a glimpse of in the mirror
after a shower or a shave, if you make it through.

It was about making it through. The body turns to grease,
as if it were moving through a bowl of grease, and heat,
and sweat like it's never known before, sweat of fear,
hatred, a lust to live simply to make the unknown die.
And sometimes a desire to die oneself, as if you live
as comic relief in some god's play, some god's joke,

a bitter, broken god, crippled by his own conceit,
turning enemies into smaller versions of yourselves.
The gun emplacement, the sudden bayonet, *are* you,
the bottom line of what you've never thought about.
And the piano wire, ingeniously strung up to meet
your face or neck, a metaphysical splitting of the atom.

Like planes above a carrier, the bugs dropped down.
Not just 'swamp angels,' the *kamikaze* 'cousins' diving
from on high, aiming for the naked arms and shoulders—
but spiders, leeches, roaches, Asian things that crawl
like enemies through mud & holes & greasy Asian sweat.
The Aussies called mosquitoes 'mossies'—something

about a breeze protecting you—there was no breeze
cooling the dirty grunts on Peleliu, Saipan, Okinawa.
Now just a few of them are left, on literal last legs,
their tattoos shriveled on collapsing wrinkled flesh.
Tattoos refer just to themselves these days—no sweat—
the needles tracing them the only pain recalled.

Piagnone In Red Hat

He liked it more when Bejing was Peking;
a little bit of peeking thrills the soul.
He liked it better when gold wasn't bling.

Now subtlety's not anybody's thing;
not everybody's clothed who's in the pool.
He liked it more when Bejing was Peking.

Cronkite had had the final word on things;
the way his mustache bounced was pretty cool.
He liked it better when gold wasn't bling.

Kennedys thought they "got it," they were kings—
but then they got it good. Dead kings don't rule.
He liked it more when Bejing was Peking.

Koufax, Gibson, could still pursue a ring;
on planes you never sat next to a mule.
He liked it better when gold wasn't bling.

The nightly news doesn't inform but clings;
the politicians take you for a fool.
He liked it more when Bejing was Peking;
he liked it better when gold wasn't bling.

Euthanasia: Poem Written on the Morning After Trump's Second Win

Spies know things. Where "the bodies are buried," all that.
National security secrets; or worse, distorted perceptions
of national security secrets. Widespread institutional fraud;
dirt on superiors. Spies are lonely lighthouses of information.

So where do they go when dementia strikes? Can't let a spy
roam free in a nursing home, where the enemy can corrupt
an attendant from, say, Kenya, into pumping a decrepit brain
about where an anti-missile-system-anti-missile-system

might be deployed near, say, Tulsa, Oklahoma—a system
that exists only to bring dollars to the good people of Tulsa
in the first place, and is good only to defend against Wichita's
escalatory threats. Soon Tulsa will have its own air force,

but the mystery is who signed off on Tulsa's blatant pork?
Is the secret locked in the brain of some blithering idiot
who wrote a political column for the Tulsa *Pulse Citizen*
before being bought off by the National Security Agency?

Or worse: the always-closing silo salesman who had an affair
with an Okie housewife, and discovered the whereabouts
of a black-ops shaft when he tried to bury the gun he used
on the wife's husband in their elaborate insurance scam?

(He was never prosecuted. Coincidence? I don't think so.
How did the rumor they're in witness protection start?)
Meanwhile, an *Oklahoma!* revival plays at the Local Theater
downtown & farmers go home sentimental about their wives.

We're all spies. We have secrets about ourselves & others
that if we're left alive too long we might blurt out in a daze
to the one relative who still comes to visit us in the home.
(She's on a fishing expedition; I wouldn't trust that one:

her travel & lodging are paid for by the one family member
who's afraid a letter might surface & throw unwanted light
on the parentage of a noble scion of the next generation,
thus influencing the ultimate dispersal of inherited funds.)

Or maybe on a hunting accident that was no accident;
or a second family in Illinois; or a third-term abortion,
even if it saved the mother's life. Humans will do *anything*,
including this visitor who is approaching now with a pillow.

Raccoon

Sometimes you feel you've overpacked your brain—
this is not the same as "thinking," so don't
imagine *hubris* as the generating engine here.
It's more like a carry-on bag for a long flight
you've stuffed with things to alleviate boredom,
only to find you never needed them because
the present presented enough life to satisfy.

The overpacking makes it hard to read sometimes;
or do anything, really. You can stare at the TV
in a dull stupor for several hours until you doze
and wake up to the sound of America screaming—
cartoon figures dancing across the headache screen,
yelling at the top of their voices they can clean
your bathtub better than you can on your best day—

like the scream of the raccoon you hit on a dark
country road in the middle of the city one night—
that followed you as you tried to flee the guilt,
knowing all the while you had to go back, finish it.
You turned around in a dark driveway, security lights
popping up, a dog barking, only to find another car
had covered your tracks, and the raccoon was dead.

III

Groves

*"I shrugged and began to walk, taking, for whatever reason,
a path through the Necropolis, and as I meandered,
I began to explain to myself what I saw,
or so I would put it, for I felt in the oddest position,
and like a stranger to my own
everyday knowledge."*

—Norman Mailer, *Ancient Evenings*

Historie Play

In the highest ranges Shakespeare excelled,
but in the lower ones he gave a whole country
referents which would serve as standards
of behavior and appearance, and allow
a nation to pare down its need for words.
The greatest art begets telepathy,
when in all hearts a common slant is thrown—
a look instead of speech, from street to throne.
Is this the reason fear resents the new,
and innocence begets antipathy:
what's not remembered is no longer known?
In the highest ranges Shakespeare
aped our outsized visions of ourselves;
but in the lower ones watched us behave.

Be Careful What You Wish For

One night as you're staring
into the 'abyss of erudition,'
the abyss loses interest in you
and moves on down the line—
sort of like metaphysical speed dating,
except you didn't get the chance
to show it your credentials.
You're ticked off, but it's unfairness
that got you here to begin with,
right? One thing you'd been certain of
was that you were an interesting case—
could this be a wake-up call?
The abyss is way down the line now,
oblivious, leaving behind a nothingness
you peek out over the rim of,
like a child who's just learned how
to stand up in his crib.

The Mind-Body Problem

Academics like to settle back into their chairs.
Sometimes they cross their legs and reach for a pipe.
Better lip or throat cancer than lung, you guess.
Cigarettes also establish a relation of hands-to-face,
but there's something odious about cigarettes,
their effects: squint-face, yellow fingertips, cough.
All humans like to do some work with their hands,
though some hands are a lot softer than others.

But getting back to those ample butts in their chairs.
Both pipes and Zippo lighters signal the long haul
of conversation is about to begin; and each erects
a literal smokescreen between the chair-man
and the scantily-clad grad student who gazes at him
with a mixture of affection and even admiration,
though deep down she suspects he's bat-shit crazy.
"Consider this," he says, trying not to look at her body

through a blue haze or a pleasant cherry cloud:
"What if you were just a brain in a vat, controlled by
an evil genius? What do you think you'd do then?"
He puffs contentedly. She knows he's about to tell her,
even as he can't help staring at her naked shoulders.
It's spring, damn it, but that should rock her back
on her heels. Nice heels, too. Rounded. How dare she
bring that body into the sacrosanct air of an office?

But he supports the young, however they wish to dress.
Or undress, as it were. And she's right: I *am* crazy.
I'm the evil genius *and* a brain in a vat. But she'd admit
she's no innocent, either: she wants what I've got—
an office on a clear spring day; the luxury of thinking
not stimulated like rats by the other evil geniuses
in the department; a chair. *She's* sure she knows what
she doesn't want: she doesn't want to kiss that cigarette-

and pipe-fouled mouth. He drones on. He repeats
his joke from class, the one about "putting Descartes
before da horse." Intuitively she knows his pun
doesn't make any sense to him, either, but he's like
an artist reaching for a connection via cleverness;
hence, the affection. She brings down the hammer:
"Didn't Wittgenstein resolve all that? Nietzsche?"
"What?" he mumbles. "Nietzsche?" He looks up

from her breasts. "I'm reaching for a connection here.
Didn't Nietzsche embody what Ludwig later codified?"
"Codify? Wittgenstein?" Trying to hide his annoyance,
he knocks his pipe against the rim of the wastebasket.
"Isn't that a *tiny* over-simplification?" Then she lands
her coup-de-grace: "OMG! I'm totally late! What*ever*!"
She jumps up. Her nipples jump up along with her.
"I forgot I have an appointment with my therapist!

Thanks, Professor!" But she doesn't leave as quickly
as would have been consistent with her agitation:
she gives him time to fix her butt in his memory.
After she's gone, he walks over to the open window
and looks down on the budding trees near Geology.

"We're all just brains in vats," he grumbles again.
He loads his seminar papers into his new backpack.
"I need a drink," he says to no one, as he walks down
the long hall, adding as he goes, "And not *only*."

The Evening Viv Carried a Sign
Outside Tom's Reading

'Good evening, Tom. I say, it's a beautiful evening, isn't it, old boy? A beautiful evening for beautiful poetry, don't you think?'

'Why, thank you, Gallagher-Phillips. That's awfully white of you.'

'Yes, yes ... 'She walks in beauty,' and all that nonsense ... Tom?'

'Yes?'

'Tom, may I have a word?'

'Of course, GP. Let's step into the back room.'

'Ah, that's better—what's that?—oh, thank you, I don't mind if I do, thank you, my good man! It's a fine establishment, Mr. Eliot, where the help follow you with a tray of drinks! What? Do I speak the truth, sir? Do I speak the truth?'

'Yes, GP, I concur wholeheartedly! The Negroid races are a veritable reservoir of talent.'

'We are lucky to have them, I say!'

'Yes, we are.'

'Tom, I, um, I suppose you noticed, ah, Vivienne, on your way in?'

'Yes, of course. Though I came in the back way. I was bringing refreshments.'

'Yes, of course, of course ... She looks awfully smart, she does. A fine-looking woman, I must say.'

'Thank you, GP. Yes, she's certainly an attractive woman.'

'Yes, she is ...'

'Is that all you wanted to say, GP?'

'What? Oh, yes, I mean, no, I wanted to ask you ...'

'Yes?'

'Well, damn the deuce, as they say! Did you happen to notice the sign?'

'The sign?'

'The sign, man, the sign!'

'I'm afraid I don't know what you mean, GP ...'

'Oh you know damn well what I mean, Tom! The sign Vivienne is carrying! The one that says "I'm the one he left behind," or some such drivel. *That* sign!'

'There is no such sign, GP.'

'What? No sign? But damn the deuce, old boy, I saw it with my own eyes! She practically shoved the damn thing in my face!'

'I'm afraid you're mistaken, GP. There was no sign. Have you read Bradley?'

'Bradley? I don't think so. Is he a poet?'

'Bradley might say the things we see come from inside us. Or something like that. "The quality of our imaginings is revealed in our interactions with others." Actually, I might have said that; I forget. I forget so much. I studied him, you know. Bradley.'

'Are you saying I simply imagined that sign? But that's preposterous! Has that green make-up seeped into your brain, old boy?'

'Frankly, GP, I'm saddened that your subconscious harbors such ill feelings toward me.'

'My *"subconscious"*?! That, that—*Jew propaganda!* I hold no such ill feelings toward you at all! Yes, it might be true I think your ideas about poetry are a bit ... *unconventional,* perhaps, but I greatly admire yourself, old boy. I apologize profusely if I've ever suggested otherwise!'

'I think we should get the evening started, don't you, Gallagher-Phillips?'

'Yes, yes, of course … I'm not imagining *you*, am I? Do you want me to tell the audience the sign that madwoman is carrying is in fact a product of their subconscious?'

'It's a beautiful evening for poetry, GP, as you said yourself. Let's leave it at that.'

Ode To Diversity

All cultures have periods of calm
in which they try to rectify the exclusionary bias
of previous activity by letting in artists and artisans
of other nationalities, races, sexual/political preferences,
even archaic religious beliefs, for God's sake,
though "religion" remains an embarrassing word.
What arises, then, is this motley mufti parti-
colored khaki nonsense the larger culture forgets

it displayed when it was a smaller culture itself.
Like in 1976, when Richard Rorty spoke to a conference
in Central America, telling the Latinx attendees
the economic engine that had built America's
high standard of living & enormous carbon footprint
was outdated, corrupt, befouled, no longer available
to them to build their own high standard of living
and enormous carbon footprint.

As you might imagine, the Latinos were pissed off,
really angry, evidently—enraged, even hurt.
So he left them to stew in their anticolonial juices,
writing poems, no doubt, that would appear years later
in revolutionary magazines abashed by lateness.
The sunset was breathtaking from the plane window—
fiery and colorful, he thought, like the people below it,
who'd bought him a first-class ticket, in anticipation.

He was a Yankee Clipper in the nineteenth century,
when previously-generous winds would die down
and the sleek symbol of trade lay becalmed for days.
There was still brass to be polished, rips in the sails,
decking to be repaired; but all that can wait a while,
as the grizzled sailor pulls out his pouch, loads his pipe,
then looks out over the calm sea with eyes as blue—
"Suh? Suh? No smoking on the plane, suh. Suh?"

Happy Hour at the Theory Lounge

"Men don't like men. Maybe it's something we were taught, or ate,
    but if you like women, you don't like men."
"Or maybe you don't like women, either."
"But wouldn't that mean you like men secretly, or unconsciously,
    or both?"
"Maybe it means you like women secretly, too—that is, after
    working through the illusion of liking them to the illusion of
    secretly liking men."
"Can you like anyone without wanting to have sex with him—uh,
    I mean, her? *It?*"
"'*They*.'"
"Right."
"Are you saying that the illusion of liking men, and the illusion of
    liking non-men, are the same as hating everybody—only
    reversed?"
"What do *you* want to reverse, my dear?"
"Maybe the *reverse* of the reverse is what we *want* to want—
    I mean, secretly—"
"So we can always consider it a game! These black leather
    accoutrement—"
"—these nipple weights you wouldn't want to hang on a
    woman because you like *her*—"
"—but which seem to be just what a man *deserves!*"
"Or, when you think about it, a woman ..."

Drinking With Grad Students

He has to let these poets, half his age,
have every way with him they hanker for;
like stuff him in a bamboo tiger cage,
or stomp his eyeballs on the barroom floor.
They think it would be fun to grind their smokes
out on his hand, carve a *stiletto* draft
between his ribs, or thread bicycle spokes
through both his balls like *shish kabobs,* and laugh.
It's just their fantasies they've trapped him in.
Tomorrow all this stuff will be forgot—
they'll get back to the rhythm of the days:
consensus that this is the "Age of Tin,"
and all of us are wise when we adopt
the cool protective-coloring of praise.

Sabbatical

After he sent a group of poems to *Condomplation*,
a journal dedicated to arts & letters and men's health,
he felt the burst of exuberance he usually felt after
he'd taken care of some professional responsibility.

So he made himself a baked potato in the microwave,
loaded it up with excessive amounts of butter & sour cream,
put on an episode of *Murder, She Wrote* and poured a Coke.
He could really kick it when he had a reason to celebrate.

Of course, he didn't really expect his poems to be accepted,
either by *Condomplation* or the mag he sent to last week,
Metacarpal Tunnel, a heavy-duty theory rag that's
beloved by review boards for summer travel grants.

He got the idea for visiting long-lost relatives in Ireland
after watching that Henry Louis Gates ancestry show
on PBS: he could whip up some slop on his heritage
and maybe get to spend the summer in an Irish pub.

At least that's the plan. Have to write some Irish poems,
but that won't be hard. He looks at an old photograph
of his great-grandmother Stoma—who couldn't write
a poem about *that* face? Sure, she's long gone by now,

but her great-grandson Oisin, or Padlock, or whatever,
might still be around; he'd be older but no doubt
still a great guide to the pubs. They say you can even
spend a night in Yeats' tower. That'd kill the board.

Naming the Animals

Back then it started out as Adam's problem,
but now we understand he always had
Eve's input, too, from the beginning.
Personally, I'm glad all that's been settled,
but we still have the problem of words.
Words are redolent of their makers;
and if you don't appreciate their makers,
the words can finally start to annoy you.

Not unlike "Adam and Eve," if you will.
Take "ableist" and "Titleist," for example.
They both refer to things in the real world,
so for that alone each one needs a name.
They don't sound that far apart, but one
is a person who has full use of his limbs—
I should have said "their" limbs, I know—
while the other is merely a golf ball.

Talk about different breeds of animals!
"Titleist" smells like Madison Avenue, right?
Or what we used to call "Madison Avenue,"
back when we were titillated by products
the new ads pushed. It has an aura about it,
wafting like an odor: "Winners" use Titleists.
Use a Titleist, and you too can be a "winner."
Win a "title" yourself. (Like, "sucker"?)

There's more. (There's always more; words
never give up.) If you don't use Titleists, well,
there's something sad about you. Pathetic.
Either you're not "in the know" (translation:
"one of us") or you just can't afford Titleists,
which do cost a bit more than the knockoffs
you pick up at the driving range. This causes
your "friends" to look away, embarrassed,

when you slice another one into the woods—
obviously, not a Titleist. Silently they agree
this will be touch-and-go when you all relax
in the clubhouse's air-conditioned leather.
The promise of a dry martini now seems a bit
whimsical as they lift their eyebrows toward
each other, trying to figure out telepathically
which one will pick up your tab as "the guest."

Words are worlds, much closer to ideograms
than you think. Take a look at "ableist."
I wonder if whoever came up with "ableist"
maybe first took a gander at "capableist"?
Most people who are "ableists" are really
"capableists"—they can do things physically
"non-ableists," much as we sympathize, can't.
And if you're really stuck on that disparity,

it's a good reason to invent the term "ableist,"
which has trace elements of bitterness in it.
But non-ableists perform tasks even ableists
fail at—so can non-ableists be "capableists"?
Or as far as grievance goes, merely "labelists"?

What does "ableism" smell like? Take a whiff:
smells like Harvard, doesn't it? I don't say
Harvard smells bad—it just smells like, well,

Harvard. "Hahvud Yahd" and all that stuff.
Not a bad smell, necessarily, but nonetheless
distinctive—next time you're in Cambridge,
stand by the front gate & breathe in deeply.
But that's neither here nor there if you need
to figure out where "ableism" comes from
and whether it figures into the connotations—
of course, it does! It took Boston centuries

to develop the smile that can dismiss you
while it voices concern about your welfare.
Boston doesn't believe in irony *about* irony,
so it assumes you don't believe in it, either.
Voices murmur in Boston, whisper along
like a quiet stream, do their makers' bidding
without scenes: mercenaries of the capable.
Even the Charles wishes it could be the Cam.

In New York, you won't hear *any* murmuring,
about drinks or anything else, least of all
your welfare. Nobody murmurs in New York;
and as far as your welfare goes, the whole bar
knows about it long before it hears "last call."
New Yorkers shout, "Over here! I'm buying!"
and while this often turns out to be untrue—
the "I'm buying" part—the crowd crowds

in together, smiling and laughing, coming up
with *bon mots*, clever puns, questionable humor,
often even commentary on what Boston's doing
these days, like "queer theory" or "ableism."
"Beantown" has a lot of theories about naming—
after all, it *is* Louis Agassiz's turf, isn't it?
Back then, Louis was the Adam of his day,
famous for his labelings of non-ableists.

Gazin' In the Grass

After the prostate is removed,
the male gaze, straight from the savannah,
turns inward, toward the clinical.
The perusal of breasts is no longer
the perusal of breasts, but the aesthetics
of proportion: how the breasts
relate to the shoulders, the neck, the chest—
the male gaze without desire
is curatorial at best.

After the prostate is removed,
the male gaze turns inward, toward the past.
"Ass" becomes memories of individuals,
the "legs for days" measure the dregs
of the heart, not the organ warming up
for the service with its cathedral tunes.
The penis still removes toxins,
but gone is the illusion of the great lover:
those days whizzed by too fast.

After the prostate is removed,
the male gaze turns inward;
for some women that's a win-win,
though the new order panics the men.
The mind still "gets" the appeal,
but the body finds it harder to feel;
and no fantasy life can spin
the predicament one finds oneself in:
the male gaze confronting the real.

Revision

If you write a good poem in life,
you will feel good about life;
and wherever you are in life
will be what the poem reflects;
and it will make you feel good
about that time; and if you go
through more times like that,
and you write more poems
that spell out these moments,
you'll be happy in those times,
too; and when you get old,
and sometimes feel a little sad,
or maybe just bluesy & quiet
on a gray winter afternoon,
you can go back & let yourself
off some hook while turning
a bitter memory on its head,
as the poem you wrote then
astonishes you with the depth
of intelligence & feeling you
hadn't realized you'd brought
to its table; and maybe it will
inspire you again as it shows
you its secret: how to fix it.

IV

[no comment]

Asylum

For a long time he was the village's only idiot.
He hung around the central cistern, usually,
or swung out over the swimming hole on the rope
the townspeople had strung up for the children.
Except he was too afraid to let go, so would swing back.
Strangely enough, that turned out to be as much fun
as splashing into the cold water, though even falling
just a few feet back on the ground, hurt. He hated water.

Everybody pretty much liked him, he thought.
He knew the townspeople didn't think he *had* thoughts,
but he thought about things once in a while.
At least he thought about things like that;
he *liked* being liked. Sure, there were days
when the children tormented him, or the adults
told him to "fuck off," whatever *that* meant.
"I don't have time for this shit," they'd say;

but when he'd answer "Shit?" they usually laughed
and patted him on the head again, so no harm done.
Once, on a day when the heat had gotten to him a little,
he'd wanted an answer, so he asked "Shit? *Shit?*"
and had even grabbed at the front of a man's coat.
That was why, as far as he could tell, the sheriff
had come to the cistern to tell him not to do that again.
"You want an explanation," he said, "but there isn't one."

He'd had no idea what the sheriff was talking about.
He tried to say he just wanted to know what "shit" meant,

but when people looked straight into his eyes he got scared,
especially when they squeezed his arm so hard it hurt.
He had bruises where the sheriff had gripped him,
and the sheriff's face had turned into the face of the man
who'd told him he didn't have time for this shit. "Shit?"
he'd said, but so softly he barely heard his own voice.

Then one morning everything changed. He hated water,
but he loved the rain, and he loved staring into the cistern
before they put the cover back on after a big downpour.
There was always a face in the water, and it was a friendly face—
it even seemed to want to know what *he* wanted to know.
When he said "Shit?" the face seemed to say "Shit?" too;
and when he laughed the face in the water laughed, too.
But that morning a second face in the water smiled up at him.

At first it scared him, and he straightened up quickly.
When he did so his elbow bumped into someone else's elbow,
and he jumped back, staring at a face that looked like
the face in the water—quickly, he looked into the cistern,
but that face was gone—and this new face smiled at him.
Somehow, this new face had come to him from the water!
The distance between himself and the word "conjure"
was too far for him to traverse in words, but he *felt* this magic.

For a long time they just stood there smiling at each other;
then the men came to put the cover back on the cistern.
When she put her hand in his as they wandered off, he trembled.
He wanted to show her the swimming hole, & the rope, & how
he swung out over the water, then back. He wanted to explain
why the water scared him, how it trapped him like the blanket
they rolled him in, his mother screaming, "I can't take it anymore!"
as they carried him to the church, to that small, scary room.

She saw the fear in his eyes, but smiled. There was no fear in hers.
She took off all her clothes & grasped the rope; almost every part
of him relaxed. She swung out over the water & let go, splashed.
He took off all his clothes, embarrassed at the part of himself
that hadn't relaxed, but she didn't mind; and soon it didn't matter,
as they played in the water and felt the warmth of the sunshine
on their naked skin. Then a sharp pain touched his shoulder, a rock
zinged his ear: some boys were throwing stones, calling them names.

He thought there must be some misunderstanding. He started
to climb up the muddy bank, but the boys shouted and ran away.
He stood there, water cascading from his hair and felt ashamed.
He'd never felt this kind of thing before. He sensed her behind him,
then she was leaning on his shoulder; for once, she seemed sad, too.
They would need food, somewhere to sleep. This time his mother
was full of love. They slept under the stars, so close to each other
their faces would have blended together, looking into a pool of water.

Gestures

Marriage begins with a Brazilian bikini wax.
You go to the beauty parlor with her the first few times.
There's a kind of secret excitement between you
when she comes out after it's finished, maybe blushing
a little, maybe giggling a little as she kisses you.
Maybe you get take-out, and all the while you're eating,
you're both thinking about that bikini wax.

It's years before you realize the bikini wax itself
was a gesture toward artifice that should have been
natural response. And that artificial excitement
was also a gesture toward what someone had told you
the exciting intimacy of marriage would be like.
Now gesture gets parsed in a thousand different ways,
as you try to determine what's reality and fantasy.

Marriage begins with a Brazilian bikini wax & ends
with a disappearance in the Amazon rainforest.
You determine your talking points early,
and prosecute them logically and articulately,
but when the time comes for action you hesitate
and lose the battle to waves of reserve troops
of gestures. Logic has no defense against gesture.

Gesture is itself a gesture against conviction.
Gesture is the recognition of the shape of conviction
sufficient to the replication of conviction's conclusions.
Gesture is placation, placebo, deflation, distraction,
diversion, misdirection, deception, placement
of deflection against the point of attack.
Logic has no defense against the strategies of gesture.

Everything's real in the Amazon rainforest; death
is most colorful here. The yellow toad's eyes seem kind—
you'll take a little kindness wherever you find it now—
but its skin is hallucinogenic poison. The microscopic
is as deadly as the leopard eyeing you from a branch.
Dreams are also gestures; you hope this is a dream.
But it's telling you that logic is a gesture, too.

Ghosted by the Zeitgeist

1

As I understand it—
but can't we say that about everything?—
getting ghosted is never hearing
from someone ever again,

but without explanation
or the finality of severance.
You think the evening out was great
but the person never contacts you

next day, or the next, or the next;
or conversely, you never notice:
the person made so little impression,
that while the evening sped on

like a pleasure boat pleasuring
the water in its richness,
you can't really remember his
or her face. The very insubstantiality

of the lights on the water,
the stars, the sensual motion
of the conversation: all that
hides, next morning, the actual

planes and shadows of the face.
Is this the preliminary of ghosting?
That you spent the evening with a ghost?
Or that your date felt the same?

2

You decide to go to the market.
Nothing connects to the corpulent world
like the market: food, goods,
people in their infinitely intricate display.

But the market of today
is not the market of yesterday
though it hangs over the bridgehead
in the same, or much the same, manner.

Huge slabs of beef used to plunge
on hooks, like Mussolini after the war.
Tongues, kidneys, whatever's inside
an animal was outside on the counters.

And the grains were in sacks,
with scoops and bags and scales.
You had to know more or less
what you wanted and how to get it.

Now everything is more discreet,
suggestive: do you want this?
Did you know you wanted this?
Yes, I can get you a tongue. How big?

Even the word "farmer" is a language
game. There are no farmers here,
only small business owners, pamphleteers—
Yes, I can get you a tongue. How big?

3

The apartment is different this morning.
Bigger, yet smaller, more of a speck.
The windows need washing on the outside.
The sun blares through them.

The market had been upsetting—
for once the freshness seemed stale,
the lettuce a little brown around the edges.
You felt like a shadow, walking.

But a shadow of what? Yourself?
And what was that "self" exactly?
Have you been *seen* lately?
The water, the stars—didn't you swim

in other eyes, effortlessly, for a few hours?
Was *it* a *he?* Or a *she?* Did it matter?
Why do *they* seem like a ghost? You begin
to think about neurological conditions,

putting one foot in front of the other,
loss of sentience. Isn't the answer
to *Why me?* always simply
Why not you? The cars go by

like years, the people like cars.
This is crazy, you think, you're still young—
you go out on *dates*, for god's sake!
Yes, I can get you a tongue. How big?

Rebound

To be the love of someone's life is good;
she said time was "redeemed," though now it's lost.
I wouldn't know, but someone I know would.

She wouldn't say to be *my* love was good,
but there was heat where now is simply frost.
So would you please explain this morning wood?

I'm sorry; I digress. That was just crude.
But every foray has collateral cost.
To be the love of someone's life is good,

but always risks the bond coming unglued;
and "mix-up" is the meaning of "star-crossed."
I wouldn't know, but someone I know would.

In olden times, this might result in blood—
lovers desire "lines in the sand," "last straws."
To be the love of someone's life was good:

a lover could be certain where he stood—
"What thou lov'st well remains; the rest is dross"—
but then somebody else's love was good.
So please explain to me this morning wood.

San Francisco, 1906

1

Nietschze said the Pre-Socratics were the true philosophers.
They were the tail end, the logical progression,
of the ancient mother-philosophy: they were the children
stepping into the sunlight, still protected by mother legs, blood;
the Furies were not yet old washer-women crones, gnarled &
    high-pitched.

Socrates said, "Know thyself" and oh with what self-approbation
do we say this to ourselves, our little butts wriggling in joy;
but already the playing field had been limited within lines.
The Sphinx still riddles us: four legs, two legs, three—
dependence, false certainty, infirmity. To know *that* self

was no bright sun, no dream of here & now, there & then,
no Apollo stepping clear of Dionysian entrails & wine.
Killing the mother after she had killed: state-sponsored vengeance
masking the turning over of an age. No wonder they were pissed:
not only one of *them*, but by the symbol, *all*.

2

My wife's mother, early on, told her I was a dreamer:
"Get out now while you still can—you've still your looks!"
Eventually, I would become her pal, her bulwark, strength.
Through everything, one listens to one's dreams,
and shows the guidons found there to one's pals.

My friend Ross said *micks, kikes* and *wops* were the talkers;
the Brits best at duplicity; the French thought they were suave;
the Germans & the Russians, god bless 'em, the *philosophes*.
"I can bear to say 'mick' but not 'kike'; you can say both. How?"
Ross said he was a novelist and novelists go listing categories—

"But when a poet says 'kike,' it comes from deep within."
I said that's hardly fair. Poets can be funny, too—irony's everywhere.
Ross looked at me and laughed. "Fair? You think it's being fair?"
I said you can't be hoarding all the humor in your private lair.
"You calling me a kike?" Ross asked. I said I wouldn't dream of it.

3

Dionysus was a door; Apollo was a mirror. You could walk into both,
but only one would let you see the world. The other was a pond.
A witch's broomtail was a pubic swatch; that's how much we
    hated them,
the ones with lively eyes, who saw around the corners of illness.
We hanged so many, sometimes pressed them to death with stone.

Women were atoms, too, were harmonies connected to the stars.
They shriveled in our eyes to crones on sticks, flying like sparks
from fires ignited by unsettling eyes we never could put out.
We called the earth 'mother,' because a woman's glance
could shake our stone foundations like a leaf. Think *Helen*.

San Francisco, April 18, 1906. 'Mother' earth had had enough.
Gold, like a beautiful woman, had borne the lust of men too long.
The crack that opened grinned a hateful grin too wide,
suspended in the dirt & fire below; and conspiratorial flames
laid waste another city, pitiful & pleading in the night.

Grave Poem for My Daughters

I wake and write a poem to my daughters,
a poem to the future, at three AM—
a time capsule they'll come upon someday.
Maybe they'll imagine my face then,
as I imagine theirs at fifty-seven tonight.
Maybe they'll suspect that on a usual day
I might wake at night, and be afraid—
afraid to leave them because the day
that was so full can never be again.
Maybe a trace of me will awaken then.

Death is suffocation, the hand opening
one last time, until you sense it's not
the hand that touched you as a child;
and in the silence there's no one left but you.
This poem is for that night, years from now,
when the thought of your own death wakes you.
I don't know what you'll feel at that moment;
maybe, for a second, you'll hear my voice.
Your memory of my voice will have to do,
as these words tonight will have to do.

Song for J.

I have been visited by angels.
You recognize an angel only in retrospect.
It's not that angels hide their splendor,
but that you find you can't negotiate
the corridor to their light.
Sometimes you run roughshod over an angel;
sometimes one offers you a door over the phone.
Sometimes you are an angel to someone else.
Perceval saw the other world when he was young,
then searched for it again until he was old.
All living requires of you a faith.
An angel brings the certainty of death;
it's often just the truth that scares you off.
Sometimes you are an angel to someone else.
I was an angel once buying a movie ticket.
The girl who sold it to me was an angel, too.
Halfway through the movie
she slipped into the seat beside me,
then we went home and made love.
For three weeks we lived where angels live.

NOTES

P 3 - This poem is for Kathy Wekselman

P 18 – This poem is for David Lehman

P 54 -'Abyss of erudition' refers to a phrase from Rabelais, concerning 'intellectuals'

P 89- This poem is for Jackie Wong

ACKNOWLEDGMENTS

Grateful acknowledgment is made to the editors of the following venues in which some of these poems first appeared:

Best American Poetry Blog
The Journal (Ohio State)

Thanks to DD, JK, MP, DP and DS, for their supportive wit and wisdom—my go-to's for encouragement.

Cover image: In the Public Domain:
Francisco Goya; "Fraile hablando con una vieja"; 1824-1825; Watercolor on ivory; Collection Princeton University Art Museum

ABOUT THE AUTHOR

 JAMES CUMMINS was born in Columbus, Ohio, in 1948, grew up in Cleveland and Indianapolis, and took degrees from the University of Cincinnati and the Iowa Writers Workshop. He's published seven books of poems, including his latest, *Recalcitrant Actors,* (Dos Madres Press, 2021), as well as poems in many journals, including the *American Poetry Review, Paris Review, Harper's, AGNI,* et al. His work appears in several anthologies, including *The Oxford Book of American Poetry, 180 More,* and five volumes of the *Best American Poetry* series. He lives in Cincinnati with his wife, the poet Maureen Bloomfield.